# Yellow in My World

## by Joanne Winne

Children's Press
A Division of Grolier Publishing
New York / London / Hong Kong / Sydney
Danbury, Connecticut

Photo Credits: All photos by Thaddeus Harden
Contributing Editors: Mark Beyer and Magdalena Alagna
Book Design: Michael DeLisio

Visit Children's Press on the Internet at:
http://publishing.grolier.com

Library of Congress Cataloging-in-Publication Data

Winne, Joanne.
    Yellow in my world / by Joanne Winne.
    p. cm. — (The world of color)
    Includes bibliographical references and index.
    Summary: A simple story highlights such yellow things as the sun, butter, and flowers.

    ISBN 0-516-23128-6 (lib. bdg.) — ISBN 0-516-23053-0 (pbk.)
    1. Yellow—Juvenile literature. [1. Yellow. 2. Color.] I. Title.

QC495.5.W568 2000
535.6—dc21
                                                      00-024382

# Contents

I am having **breakfast**.

Can you count the yellow foods?

5

Eggs are yellow.

The butter on my **toast** is yellow, too.

7

I help my mother in the **garden**.

I wear **gloves** and a hat.

How many yellow things am I wearing?

9

I am wearing four yellow things.

My gloves and hat are yellow.

My socks and shirt are yellow, too.

11

We gather flowers in the garden.

Do you know the name of the yellow flowers?

**Tulips** are yellow.

14

15

Mom brings us a cool drink.

Can you guess what drink is made from a yellow fruit?

17

**Lemonade** is made from lemons.

Lemons are yellow.

19

Yellow is everywhere.

What do you see around you that is yellow?

# New Words

breakfast  (**brehk**-fast) a meal eaten in the morning

garden  (**gar**-din) a place where flowers can grow

gloves (**gluhvz**) coverings for the hands

lemonade  (**leh**-muh-**nayd**) a sweet drink made from lemons

toast  (**tohst**)  bread that has been cooked until it is brown

tulips (**too**-lips) a kind of flower

# To Find Out More

**Books**
*Orchard's Little Yellow Book of Nursery Rhymes*
by Nila Aye
Orchard Books

*Purple, Green and Yellow*
by Helene Desputeaux, Robert N. Munsch
Firefly Books

**Web Site**
**Crayola**
http://www.crayola.com
The official Crayola Web site. It has a lot of pictures
to print and color. It also has crafts, games, and 23
online art.

# Index

About the Author
Joanne Winne taught fourth grade for nine years. She currently writes and edits books for children. She lives in Hoboken, New Jersey.

Reading Consultants
Kris Flynn, Coordinator, Small School District Literacy, The San Diego County Office of Education

Shelly Forys, Certified Reading Recovery Specialist, W.J. Zahnow Elementary School, Waterloo, IL

Peggy McNamara, Professor, Bank Street College of Education, Reading and Literacy Program